# Ignatian Rosary

## A Jesuit Way to Pray
## a Dominican Devotion

Leo-Martin Angelo R. Ocampo, OP

D1447144

Liguori

*Imprimi Potest*:
Stephen T. Rehrauer, CSsR, Provincial
Denver Province, the Redemptorists

Published by Liguori Publications, Liguori, Missouri 63057.
To order, call 800-325-9521, or visit Liguori.org.

ISBN: 978-0-7648-2856-0

Cover image: Immaculate/Shutterstock

Printed in the United States of America • First Edition
25 24 23 22 21 / 5 4 3 2 1

# Contents

## About the Author

**Leo-Martin Angelo R. Ocampo, OP,** a published author, is at the Center for Theology, Religious Studies and Ethics at the Pontifical and Royal University of Santo Tomás in Manila, where he is a faculty member at the Institute of Religion, the academic collaborations officer of the ecclesiastical faculties, and a research associate at the Center for Theology, Religious Studies and Ethics at the Pontifical and Royal University of Santo Tomás in Manila. He is finishing his doctoral studies in theology at the university. His master's degree is in theological studies and his bachelor's degree is in philosophy.

# Acknowledgments

My deep and heartfelt gratitude goes to my Jesuit mentors at San José Seminary, Loyola School of Theology, Ateneo de Manila University, and to my Dominican family in the Sanctus Dominicus Lay Dominican Fraternity and the Pontifical University of Santo Tomas in Manila. Being a son of these two great spiritual traditions is a rare gift for which I will always be thankful to the Lord. Special thanks to dear friends in the Lord who helped improve this booklet: Fr. Victor de Jesus, SJ; Fr. Joseph Don Zaldivar; and Vince Salles. I thank Liguori Publications for producing this pamphlet during the Dominican and Ignatian Jubilee Year, a time also significant for the rosary: 2021 is the 450th anniversary of the miraculous victory of Christian forces in Lepanto in 1571, which Pope St. Pius V attributed to Mary's intercession.

*To Dominic and Ignatius as we celebrate 2021–22, a Jubilee both Dominican and Ignatian: the 500th anniversary of Ignatius' conversion, the 400th anniversary of his canonization, and the 800th year of the birth of Dominic into life eternal.*

## Introduction

The title of this pamphlet may raise questions, like, "What is an Ignatian-style rosary?" And how can "a Jesuit way to pray" be applied to "a Dominican devotion"? Traditionally, a rivalry exists between the Jesuits and the Dominicans, not only in jokes and other friendly ways but in history. Having the Church's top theologians among the ranks of both orders has led to frequently unavoidable debates and disagreements. Also, as religious orders known for providing quality education, their universities and schools have always vied for supremacy in prestige and performance. Despite this reality, these two great traditions need not always be in conflict.

After all, did not Ignatius' conversion begin with a desire to emulate Francis and Dominic? The content found within these pages is an effort to fuse the richness of two great spiritual traditions. It seeks to apply Ignatian principles and techniques—especially imaginative contemplation—to the rosary, a Dominican prayer that is both familiar and dear to many Catholics.

And how providential to publish this pamphlet in 2021, a time when both orders are celebrating important Jubilees, plus the miraculous Christian victory that took place 450 years ago, all of which I noted on the page of acknowlegments.

To Ignatius, prayer is a form of exercise, no different from physical exercise. The more regularly we do it, the better we become at doing it, and the more benefit we gain. He titled his masterpiece *The Spiritual Exercises* so it would be seen as a guide for those who want to become closer to God. Unfortunately, not all people have the time, money, or opportunity to do the full Spiritual Exercises that ideally last for about thirty days, as Ignatius designed it. Seldom, too, are people able to go on retreats of five or eight days. However, most of us—perhaps with some extra effort—would be able to set aside thirty minutes to an hour of quality time each day to pray. Combining the Ignatian method of contemplation with the daily praying of the rosary can thus be a way of doing the retreat in daily life, making it more accessible to the lay faithful.

The rosary once earned the moniker "the ordinary person's breviary." Perhaps with the help of this booklet, the holy rosary also could become known as "the ordinary person's retreat."

# Ignatian Contemplation

*Contemplation* is a word used infrequently in daily conversation. The *Oxford English Dictionary* offers a wide range of definitions, from "look at thoughtfully for a long time" to "think about deeply and at length." Yet the dictionary fails to capture what contemplation means in the spiritual sense. Moreover, the word is often confined to the realm of mysticism, an obscure field most often associated with the saints and spiritual elite and into which most of us mere mortals would not dare dabble. Even among religious people, it can carry different nuances. For instance, a Carmelite or Jesuit will not mean exactly the same thing when using the word. For clarity, we can apply the definition Ignatius gives to the word *contemplation* in *The Spiritual Exercises of St. Ignatius* (1522–24):

> *[To take] the true groundwork of the narrative, and [through] discussing and considering for himself, find something which makes the events a little clearer or brings*

*them a little more home to him—whether this comes through his own reasoning or because his intellect is enlightened by the Divine power—he will get more spiritual relish and fruit than if the one who is giving the Exercises had much explained and amplified the meaning of the events. For it is not knowing much, but realizing and relishing things interiorly, that contents and satisfies the soul.*

In other words, Ignatian contemplation involves entering the biblical narrative and exploring its depths using one's mind with the help of God's grace. For example, while dealing with episodes in the life of Christ, one does not just read and ponder an explanation of an episode of Christ from a third party, but one experiences it personally by employing the creativity of imagination, thus making it clearer to the mind and closer to the heart.

As with any exercise, this activity takes some skill, which is learned and developed by frequent repetition. At first, one may have difficulty imagining the story. That is where aids and suggestions, such as those provided in this booklet, can be helpful. Over time and with enough patience, the "black-and-white photos" of stories and prayers will start to come alive with color, sounds, smell, or even sensation. One slowly finds oneself not just watching but engaging in scenes and taking part in them—not as a spectator but as a participant.

Brief points for consideration are provided to help the reader enter more fully into each mystery and follow as closely as possible the points that Ignatius himself provides in *The Spiritual Exercises*. These should be treated as pointers rather than prescriptions. While it is good for you to stay close to the points, it is unnecessary to be limited or confined by them. Also, you need not cover all the points for each mystery. Choosing one or two points you feel drawn to is sufficient. In matters of prayer, follow the lead of the good spirit who may wish you to contemplate some other aspect of the mystery. Be open.

The objective to know and understand can be ensured efficiently through study and reflection. The ultimate goal is to feel and savor, which is what Ignatius means by "not knowing much, but realizing and relishing things interiorly." He does not mean to forsake knowledge and understanding, both of which are important in our relationship with God—for "it is by knowing that comes loving," as St. Thomas Aquinas says.

Rather, St. Ignatius invites us to develop familiarity with God on an equally important and complementary level—that of the heart. The phrase just quoted has been condensed into an idiom much loved in Ignatian circles: *non multa sed multum* ("many but not much"). Simply, it means that the quantity of knowledge or insight we have about God is not as important as the depth of closeness we attain with him.

# The Rosary as a
# Prayer of the Heart

This guide endeavors to assist you in making the rosary a prayer of the heart. For some, the rosary can be a prayer that is merely recited or said, not contemplated. Others move ahead by reflecting or meditating on the mysteries of the rosary as a form of "mental" prayer. Thus, it can become what Pope St. John Paul II aptly described as the "school of Mary" where we can "contemplate the beauty on the face of Christ and experience the depths of his love," bringing out the Christocentric character and experiential dynamic of this Marian devotion (On the Most Holy Rosary [*Rosarium Virginis Mariae*], 1). As with any school, the more effort that you, the student, give, the more you will learn. Thus, it is worthwhile to bear in mind Ignatius' advice to engage in spiritual exercises "with great courage and generosity," opening yourself as fully as possible to God.

In the spirit St. John Paul II outlines, this pamphlet will apply the Ignatian technique of imaginative contemplation and strive to help you experience the mysteries of the day. Start your contemplation with a composition in which you imagine the setting where the mystery is about to take place. Slowly let the story unfold, guided by the points provided and your knowledge of biblical narratives. Little by little, you will learn to employ each of the different senses of your soul: spiritual sight, hearing, touch, and even smell and taste. Ideally, with continual practice, you will improve at this form of prayer. The vocal prayers here should not be repeated by rote. Rather, the repetition should be a kind of mantra, much like the Jesus Prayer in the Orthodox tradition that creates a stable rhythm and helps you to enter deeply into silence and contemplation.

This method is both intensely Ignatian and deeply Dominican. Such was the insight of the great painter and mystic of the Order of Preachers, Fra Angelico, when the Dominican painted scenes in the life of Christ and our Lady in the cells of the brethren at the Priory of San Marco in Florence. He depicted characters in the Gospel stories and the figure of Dominic—at times along with other saints—as part of the scene. The invitation to the friar inhabiting the cell bid him to enter the scene and become part of it, just like Dominic and the saints.

This type of devotion to the rosary will take some time and is best done alone. Giving it your best effort will require time, attention, and being mindful of avoiding shortcuts that Ignatius warns can hinder spiritual growth. While daily prayer will follow the ebb and flow of life, with high and low points, we must always strive to not give in to laziness and mediocrity in prayer. The more tempted you may be to cut corners, the more we ought to muster our might to pray.

Aside from contemplation, the petition is also introduced at the beginning of the rosary, corresponding to the *id quod volo* ("that which I desire") in the Spiritual Exercises or the grace that is being desired. Likewise, a conversation is suggested at the end of the prayer period corresponding to the triple colloquy. These two elements that frame the prayer period are highly important because they engage you and—as you learn to listen to God—make prayer a real two-way conversation.

## Entering into Prayer

Before you begin, arrange your prayer space in a manner that will help you pray better. Ignatius meticulously describes how to set up prayer space. You can start by choosing a quiet area in your home that is conducive to relaxation, with a comfortable chair, a mat if you prefer to be on the floor, or a *prie-dieu* ("prayer desk").

Your body's position—standing, sitting, or kneeling—can vary but your inner disposition should always be focused and attentive. Dominic adopted various postures in prayer, as observed by those who knew him well. Different postures helped his prayer to become more holistic, involving not only the mind and the soul but the body and whole being. Avoid being rushed. Make your time with the Lord quality time.

As an added aid to prayer, you may want to have a simple altar where you place an icon or image on which you focus your gaze. You might also like to light a candle, play music that helps enhance the mood, or add a soothing scent. In time, you may want to introduce variations in the elements in keeping with the mysteries of the day. For instance, you may wish to add flowers for the joyful mysteries, more candles for the luminous mysteries, dim the lights for the sorrowful mysteries, or have the room all lit up for the glorious mysteries. Once again, the Ignatian principle *non multa sed multum* applies. It is not about the quantity but the quality of things you add and the interior disposition it helps to create within your soul. Your prayer space need not and should not be grandiose. However, Ignatius notes that it is of utmost importance to get as much privacy and quiet as possible. Solitude pleases God, enables you to focus on godly things versus distractions, and makes you more intimate with the Lord.

Last, as the lovely Dominican motto goes, *contemplari et contemplata aliis tradere*, which means "to hand down to others the fruits of contemplation." Prayer does not stop at entering the heart of the Gospel but continues as you naturally share it with others in whatever ways you can. To quote the apostles: "It is impossible for us not to speak about what we have seen and heard" (Acts 4:20). Always enter into prayer, but never leave it. Instead, allow it to permeate your life and energize your own mission. As you grow daily in familiarity with Jesus by being immersed in this school of Mary that is the rosary, may all be able to say with St. John:

*What was from the beginning,*
  *what we have heard,*
  *what we have seen with our eyes,*
  *what we looked upon*
  *and touched with our hands*
  *concerns the Word of life—*

*for the life was made visible;*
  *we have seen it and testify to it and*
  *proclaim to you the eternal life*
  *that was with the Father and was made*
    *visible to us—*

*what we have seen and heard*
  *we proclaim now to you,*
  *so that you too may have fellowship with us;*
  *for our fellowship is with the Father*
  *and with his Son, Jesus Christ (1 John 1:1–3).*

*What was from the beginning,*
*what we have heard,*
*what we have seen with our eyes,*
*what we looked upon*
*and touched with our hands*
*concerns the Word of life.*

1 John 1:1

# Introductory Prayers

## BECOMING AWARE OF GOD'S PRESENCE

Once you have prepared or approved your sacred space, begin your prayer, as Ignatius advises, "a step or two [in front of] the place where I have to contemplate or meditate, I will put myself standing for the space of an Our Father, my intellect raised on high, considering how God our Lord is looking at me, and I will make an act of reverence or humility." I suggest you make a slow, deep bow, followed by the Sign of the Cross.

## THE SIGN OF THE CROSS

*In the name of the Father, and of the Son, and of the Holy Spirit. Amen.*

### *ID QUOD VOLO* (PETITION)

As Ignatius suggests, begin your prayer period by stating the specific grace that you desire to obtain from God. More than just material favors, graces mean spiritual gifts. Graces patterned after those in the Spiritual Exercises are suggested below, in keeping with the mysteries that will be prayed for the day, to which may be added other particular graces that you wish to beg from God.

In this prayer period, I beg for the grace...

**Joyful Mysteries**

to be joyful with Jesus and Mary (and...)

**Luminous Mysteries**

to be closer to Jesus and Mary (and...)

**Sorrowful Mysteries**

to feel pain and sorrow with Jesus and Mary (and...)

**Glorious Mysteries**

to rejoice with Jesus and Mary (and...)

## THE APOSTLES' CREED

*I believe in God,*
*the Father almighty,*
*Creator of heaven and earth,*
*and in Jesus Christ, his only Son, our Lord,*
*who was conceived by the Holy Spirit,*
*born of the Virgin Mary,*
*suffered under Pontius Pilate,*
*was crucified, died and was buried;*
*he descended into hell;*
*on the third day he rose again from the dead;*
*he ascended into heaven,*
*and is seated at the right hand of God*
        *the Father almighty;*
*from there he will come to judge*
*the living and the dead.*

*I believe in the Holy Spirit,*
*the holy catholic Church,*
*the communion of saints,*
*the forgiveness of sins,*
*the resurrection of the body,*
*and life everlasting.*
*Amen.*

The Apostles' Creed is followed by one Our Father, three Hail Marys, and one Glory Be.

## THE OUR FATHER

*Our Father, who art in heaven,*
*hallowed be thy name;*
*thy kingdom come;*
*thy will be done on earth as it is in heaven.*
*Give us this day our daily bread;*
*and forgive us our trespasses*
*as we forgive those who trespass against us;*
*and lead us not into temptation,*
*but deliver us from evil.*
*Amen.*

## THE HAIL MARY

*Hail Mary, full of grace, the Lord is with thee;*
*blessed art thou amongst women,*
*and blessed is the fruit of thy womb, Jesus.*
*Holy Mary, Mother of God,*
*pray for us sinners*
*now and at the hour of our death.*
*Amen.*

## THE GLORY BE (The Doxology)

*Glory be to the Father,*
*and to the Son,*
*and to the Holy Spirit.*
*As it was in the beginning,*
*is now,*
*and ever shall be,*
*world without end.*
*Amen.*


Follow the prayers with the contemplation of
the mysteries of the day:


On Mondays and Saturdays,
   the five Joyful Mysteries:

   The Annunciation
   The Visitation
   The Nativity
   The Presentation in the Temple
   The Finding in the Temple

On Thursdays, the five Luminous Mysteries:

The Baptism of Christ in the Jordan
The Wedding Feast at Cana
Jesus' Proclamation of the Coming
   of the Kingdom of God
The Transfiguration
The Institution of the Eucharist

On Tuesdays and Fridays,
   the five Sorrowful Mysteries:

The Agony in the Garden
The Scourging at the Pillar
The Crowning with Thorns
The Carrying of the Cross
The Crucifixion and Death

On Wednesdays and Sundays (outside the
   season of Lent, Advent, and Christmas), the
   five Glorious Mysteries:

The Resurrection
The Ascension
The Descent of the Holy Spirit
The Assumption
The Coronation of Mary

On Sundays during Advent and Christmas,
  use the Joyful Mysteries

On Sundays during Lent,
  use the Sorrowful Mysteries.

Pray the Our Father on the first large bead, followed by the points as a short introduction to the mystery to guide your contemplation.

Then, on each of the next ten beads, pray a Hail Mary. While pronouncing these prayers, continue to contemplate the mystery in the life of Jesus and Mary.

At the end of a decade of ten Hail Marys, pray the Glory Be and the Fatima Prayer.

### THE FATIMA PRAYER

*O my Jesus, forgive us our sins, save us from the fires of hell; lead all souls to Heaven, especially those in most need of thy mercy.*

During the paschal triduum, the Glory Be is traditionally replaced by this:

On Holy Thursday

**V.** Christ was made obedient for us.
**R.** Even unto death.

On Good Friday

**V.** Christ was made obedient for us even unto
death.
**R.** Even death on a cross.

On Holy Saturday

**V.** Christ was made obedient for us even unto
death, even death on a cross.
**R.** For which God has greatly exalted Him and
bestowed on Him a name above every other
name.

This process continues through each of the five decades and ends with the concluding prayers.

All five mysteries are usually contemplated in one prayer period. Alternatively, in keeping with Ignatius' advice, you may also choose to stay in one specific mystery or another from which you derive consolation and nourishment at the moment, "as long as you find meanings, comparisons, relish and consolation" without hurrying on to the next. This "alternative" is not entirely new because it has always been possible to say only one decade or any number of decades of the rosary in one prayer period. For example, if you find great comfort in meditating on the annunciation at a given moment, you can choose to focus on that mystery for the whole prayer period.

Another possibility especially appropriate on feast days such as March 25 (Annunciation) or August 22 (Queenship of Mary) is to focus on a particular mystery for the whole duration of five decades, after which you also end the period in the usual way. Again, this is not entirely new. This method of praying the rosary also is found in *The Golden Manual*, a devotional from the 1700s.

*For the life was made visible;*
*we have seen it and testify to it and*
*proclaim to you the eternal life*
*that was with the Father and was*
*made visible to us.*

1 John 1:2

# The Joyful Mysteries

*On Mondays, Saturdays,
and the Sundays of Advent
and Christmas*

# First Joyful Mystery
## *The Annunciation*

Pray the Our Father and consider this:

Behold with the eyes of your soul the Trinity in heaven as they look down with mercy on all the people suffering on earth. Listen with the ears of your soul as they decide to send the Son. Despite knowing what this would entail, the Father says yes, and the Son gives his own yes to the Father in their infinite union of love who is the Holy Spirit. Be with Mary in her room in Nazareth as the Angel Gabriel is sent to bring the news to her. Join her as she, despite her fear and hesitation, boldly gives her yes to God in turn. In the union of these affirmations, "the Word became flesh and made his dwelling among us" (John 1:14).

As you pray ten Hail Marys, share in Mary's total surrender to God's will and adore Christ, the eternal Son of God, newly made man in her womb for love of you and to save you. End with the Glory Be in trust and obedience.

## Second Joyful Mystery
### *The Visitation*

Pray the Our Father and consider this:

See how Mary is filled with compassion upon learning of her elderly cousin's pregnancy and hurries to be with her in this difficult time. Be there as Elizabeth and the child in her womb are filled with joy in the presence of God himself in Mary's womb. Mary, too, is overcome with joy at witnessing God's action in their lives and breaks into song: "My soul proclaims the greatness of the Lord, my spirit rejoices in God my savior" (Luke 1:46–47). Stay with Mary as she remains for three more months to help her cousin before returning to her home.

As you pray the ten Hail Marys, bask with joy like Elizabeth and John in the presence of Mary and of the Word made flesh in her womb. As she did with Elizabeth, she is also here to be with you and to help you in whatever you may be going through. Let her invite you to visit and help your own "Elizabeth." In thanksgiving and generosity, end with the Glory Be.

## Third Joyful Mystery
### *The Birth of Our Lord*

Pray the Our Father and consider this:

Find yourself in the stable with Mary, Joseph, and the newborn Child. See the poverty in which the Lord has chosen to be born for you. This family is poor in almost everything, even things considered basic and essential, like proper shelter and health care. And yet they do have what is most necessary: they have each other, and they have Jesus. Behold the little Child in the manger, born for you on this holy night. See him smile as the angels sing, "Glory to God in the highest and on earth peace to those on whom his favor rests" (Luke 2:14).

As you pray the ten Hail Marys, share in the joy of Mary and Joseph as they gaze with love at the Baby Jesus and caress him. In the cold and barren stable, allow yourself to be enfolded in the embrace of the Holy Family. In gratitude and love, end with the Glory Be.

## Fourth Joyful Mystery
### *The Presentation of the Child Jesus in the Temple*

Pray the Our Father and consider this:

Go to the Temple with Joseph and Mary as they present the Child to the Father. In their poverty, all they can afford to offer is a pair of turtledoves. But those with spiritual eyes immediately recognize the incomparable treasure they had. The "righteous and devout" Simeon, who has waited his entire life for this moment, finally sees the Savior. Holding him in his arms, he exclaims, "Now, Master, you may let your servant go in peace, according to your word, for my eyes have seen your salvation" (Luke 2:25, 29–30). Also after seeing Jesus, the prophetess Anna "gave thanks to God and spoke about the child to all who were awaiting the redemption of Jerusalem" (Luke 2:38).

As you pray the ten Hail Marys, ask Mary and Joseph if you can also cradle the Child in your arms as Simeon and Anna did. Let the Child embrace you and satisfy all your heart's desires. In awe and adoration, end with the Glory Be.

## Fifth Joyful Mystery
### *Finding Jesus in the Temple*

Pray the Our Father and consider this:

Share in the anguish and anxiety of Mary and Joseph as they look for Jesus, who has been lost for three days. What relief to find him safe in the Temple, sitting and talking with the teachers! Many times, in our life, we also long for the Lord's presence, and what joy it is to find him again! Mary tells Jesus that they were terribly worried, but he gives an answer that they don't understand. Still, what is important now is that they are reunited, they return home together as one family, "and his mother kept all these things in her heart" (Luke 2:51).

As you pray the ten Hail Marys, contemplate Jesus sitting among the teachers with Mary and Joseph. Let all your worries, anxieties, and fears of the moment vanish in his presence. We do not always understand his ways, but it is enough to see that he is here with you. In trust and hope, end with the Glory Be.

# The Luminous Mysteries

*On Thursdays*

## First Luminous Mystery
### *The Baptism of the Lord*

Pray the Our Father and consider this:

Be there as Christ bids Mother Mary farewell to begin his ministry. Follow him as he heads to the Jordan River for his baptism by John. Go with him into the water as he falls in line with ordinary people to receive this baptism of repentance. John himself is unwilling to baptize Jesus who does not need any baptism, but the Lord wants to be one with us in all things. Be baptized with him and with the rest of the crowd. And now, watch as the heavens open, and the Holy Spirit descends on him in bodily form, like a dove. Listen to the voice from heaven telling him: "You are my beloved Son; with you I am well pleased" (Luke 3: 22).

As you pray the ten Hail Marys, remain with Jesus who has just been baptized. Feel his deep intimacy with the Father and the Holy Spirit that he wants to share with you and with all humanity. In praise and worship, end with the Glory Be.

## Second Luminous Mystery
### *The Wedding at Cana*

Pray the Our Father and consider this:

Join Jesus, Mary, and the disciples as they grace a wedding feast at Cana. In the middle of the festivities, the wine runs out, potentially causing a big disgrace to the newlywed couple. Observe how Mary is quick to sense the problem and approach her Son. At first, Jesus refuses to get involved, saying that his hour has not yet come, yet Mary still directs the servants to Jesus: "Do whatever he tells you" (John 2:5). Look at how they do as Jesus said, filling six stone jars with water, even though they didn't understand why. Behold how he turns that water into the best of wine and see the disciples believe in him.

As you pray the ten Hail Marys, entrust your cares to Mary and let her bring them all to Jesus. Allow Mary to lead you to Jesus and tell you, in your own anxieties and problems, what she told the servants: "Do whatever he tells you." Listen to Jesus as he speaks to you in your heart and tells you what you must do. In trust and obedience, end with the Glory Be.

## Third Luminous Mystery
### *The Proclamation of the Good News*

Pray the Our Father and consider this:

Follow Jesus as he goes to the different towns and villages, proclaiming the kingdom of God. Choose a favorite Gospel scene to focus on during this mystery. Listen as he teaches the crowds or narrates the parables. Be there as he heals the sick, casts out demons, or feeds the big crowd. Witness one of many miracles. Observe how he deals with sinners and calls them to repentance. Join the apostles as they ask him questions or simply share some light moments with him. Heed the invitation of Jesus to take up your cross and follow him.

As you pray the ten Hail Marys, remain with Jesus as you contemplate your chosen Gospel scene. Immerse yourself as fully as possible in the story. As you do this, allow Jesus to bring the kingdom of God into your own life now as well. In faith and love, end with the Glory Be.

## Fourth Luminous Mystery
### *The Transfiguration*

Pray the Our Father and consider this:

Go up to Mount Tabor with Jesus, along with Peter, James, and John. Behold our Lord as he is transfigured before your eyes, his face becoming brighter than the sun and his garments white as snow. See him converse with Moses and Elijah and let the cloud of the presence of God enfold you. Peter was beginning to suggest staying there, but a voice spoke from the cloud, saying: "This is my beloved Son, with whom I am well pleased; listen to him" (Matthew 17:5). Seeing how the disciples were completely terrified, Jesus goes to them and touches them, saying: "Rise, and do not be afraid" (Matthew 17:7).

As you pray the ten Hail Marys, be with Jesus and the disciples on Mount Tabor as you experience the transfiguration. Allow Jesus to touch you and strengthen your faith just as he did for the disciples. Despite any challenges that lie ahead in your life, God remains in control, and victory is certain. In adoration and trust, end with the Glory Be.

## Fifth Luminous Mystery
### *The Institution of the Eucharist*

Pray the Our Father and consider this:

Enter into the upper room where Jesus is about to celebrate the Passover meal with his disciples. Listen as he tells you of his imminent death, with one of you about to betray him. Be there as he washes everyone's feet. Do not protest like Peter but allow him to wash yours, too. Watch how he takes the bread, blesses it, breaks it and gives it for you to partake, inviting all of you to "take and eat; this is my body." See how he takes the wine, blesses it, and gives it for you to drink, saying, "Drink from it, all of you, for this is my blood of the covenant" (Matthew 26:27–28). After the meal, Judas betrays the Lord, but the heart of Jesus goes out to him.

As you pray the ten Hail Marys, remain with Jesus and the disciples. Allow our Lord to express his love for you by washing your feet and nourishing you with his own Body and Blood in the Eucharist. Feel his love, even in those times when we are unfaithful to him. In humility and thanksgiving, end with the Glory Be.

# The Sorrowful Mysteries

*On Tuesdays, Fridays, and the Sundays of Lent*

## First Sorrowful Mystery
### *The Agony in the Garden*

Pray the Our Father and consider this:

Go with Jesus and his disciples to the Garden of Gethsemane. Stay with him as Jesus becomes greatly distressed and troubled at his imminent passion and death. So terrible is his pain and agony that he says, "My soul is sorrowful even to death" (Mark 14:34). "His sweat became like drops of blood falling on the ground" (Luke 22:44). His great trial of faith had begun, and as a human, he trembled before what he was about to undergo. But the more anguish he feels, the more he prays, surrendering himself completely to the Father's will. Join your heart to his as he says, "Father, if you are willing, take this cup away from me; still, not my will but yours be done" (Luke 22:42).

As you pray the ten Hail Marys, stay with Jesus in his agony. Be one with him as he struggles to overcome his fear and conform his will to the will of the Father. In trust and love, end with the Glory Be.

## Second Sorrowful Mystery
### *The Scourging at the Pillar*

Pray the Our Father and consider this:

Follow Jesus into the courtyard of Pilate. He is now weak, tired, and in pain after endless interrogation and torture. None among the courts of the chief priests, Herod, or Pilate are able to convict him. And not one has the honesty and courage to acquit him. Now, in an attempt to satisfy the angry mob, Pilate orders Jesus to be scourged. The Roman flagellum is a very cruel device, designed to inflict terrible pain, with sharp edges that are meant to tear into the flesh with every lash. Watch and pray as Jesus endures all of this out of love for you.

As you pray the ten Hail Marys, remain with Jesus as he undergoes this excruciatingly painful scourging. Feel his love by which he endures all of this suffering to save you from your sins. In sorrow and repentance, end with the Glory Be.

## Third Sorrowful Mystery
### *The Crowning with Thorns*

Pray the Our Father and consider this:

Stay with Jesus, who is in horrible pain after being scourged. Not content with just physical abuse, the cruel soldiers proceed to torment him psychologically and emotionally by mocking and insulting him. See them weave a crown of long and sharp thorns and put it on his head. Then they put a purple cloak on him, spit on him, and shout, "Hail, king of the Jews!" Watch as they bring him out to Pilate, who knows that he is innocent but gives in to the ruthless crowd that is clamoring, "Crucify him! Crucify him!" Listen closely as Pilate, washing his hands of guilt, condemns Jesus to death.

As you pray the ten Hail Marys, be with Jesus as he patiently bears all this insult and humiliation without grumbling, like a lamb being led to the slaughter. He bears everything out of obedience to the Father and out of compassion for poor sinners. In humility and contrition for your sins, end with the Glory Be.

## Fourth Sorrowful Mystery
### *The Carrying of the Cross*

Pray the Our Father and consider this:

Follow Jesus as he embraces the cross and heads to Calvary. See how his body has been weakened by torture and fatigue, but his mind and spirit remain strong and determined to fulfill the Father's will to save poor sinners. As he is barely able to bear the weight of the wood, remain close to him as he inches slowly down the streets of Jerusalem, tottering under the heavy load. Three times he falls, and three times he struggles to get up, until he can do no more. The soldiers then grab a passerby named Simon and force him to carry the cross for Jesus.

As you pray the ten Hail Marys, meet Jesus on the way together with Mary and stay as close as possible to Jesus as he carries the cross. Feel his heart as he takes each step on the way to Calvary out of love for the Father and for you. If you wish, be Simon and carry the cross with him. In sorrow and gratitude, end with the Glory Be.

## Fifth Sorrowful Mystery
### *The Crucifixion and Death of Jesus*

Pray the Our Father and consider this:

Stay as close as possible to Jesus as you arrive in Calvary and witness the soldiers nailing him to the cross. Listen intently to what he says in these final moments and ponder them in your heart. Behold him as he falls into a long and deafening silence, slowly being drained of his blood and running out of breath. As darkness begins to cover the place, hear him as he breaks the silence with a piercing cry of deep, all-encompassing pain: "My God, my God, why have you forsaken me?" (Matthew 27:46, Mark 15:34, and see Psalm 22). Feel him breathe his last breath as he surrenders his spirit to the hands of the Father. See what he has done for you and feel how much he loves you!

As you pray the ten Hail Marys, stand with Mary, along with John and the women disciples, as you accompany Jesus to the end. Be one with him in his pain and anguish, and share in his total self-surrender to the Father. In gratitude and love, end with the Glory Be.

# The
# Glorious
# Mysteries

*On Wednesdays and Sundays*

## First Glorious Mystery
### *The Resurrection*

Pray the Our Father and consider this:

Be in the room with Mary as her risen Son visits and comforts her in all her grief and suffering. Rise with the women early, before sunrise, and go visit his tomb only to find it empty. Gaze with the eyes of your heart at the empty tomb and hear the angel say, "He is not here, but he has been raised" (Luke 24:6). Accompany Mary Magdalene, her eyes flowing with tears, as she looks for his body and meets him in the garden as you hear him call your name. Join the disciples huddled in the upper room, walking to Emmaus, or fishing in the Sea of Galilee as Jesus appears to them. Allow the risen Lord to engage you in intimate conversation as he did Peter, healing you from your past and forgiving your sins.

As you pray the ten Hail Marys, rejoice in the victory of the risen Lord as you contemplate one of the resurrection accounts mentioned above. Let him take away all your fear and sadness and fill your heart with joy and peace. In praise and thanksgiving, end with the Glory Be.

## Second Glorious Mystery
### *The Ascension of Jesus into Heaven*

Pray the Our Father and consider this:

Go with the disciples to the Mount of Olives and meet Jesus. Receive his blessing with the disciples. Take to heart the mission he entrusts to you to bring the Good News wherever you go. As you watch Jesus ascend up to heaven, slowly disappearing among the clouds, allow him to assure you: "And behold, I am with you always, until the end of the age" (Matthew 28:20). Then greet the two angels who appear and say: "Why are you standing there looking at the sky? This Jesus who has been taken up from you into heaven will return in the same way as you have seen him going into heaven" (Acts 1:11).

As you pray the ten Hail Marys, contemplate Jesus as he is taken to heaven. Let his words of assurance sink in as you commit yourself to the mission he entrusted to you: to share his message with everyone you encounter in your daily life. Although you may not see him, he is always with you and will come back for you one day. In trust and love, end with the Glory Be.

## Third Glorious Mystery
### *The Descent of the Holy Spirit*

Pray the Our Father and consider this:

Remain in the upper room to be one in prayer with Mary and the other disciples as they await the coming of the Holy Spirit promised by Jesus. Be there when the entire house is suddenly filled with a sound like a mighty rushing wind. See the tongues of fire as they appear and rest on each one of you. Open your heart and your whole self to the Holy Spirit. Allow the Holy Spirit to flood your soul and your whole being.

As you pray the ten Hail Marys, become one with Mary and the other disciples as they experience the coming of the Holy Spirit. Receive the Holy Spirit and allow him to shower your heart with his gifts, especially the ones that you need most at this point in your life. In adoration and surrender, end with the Glory Be.

## Fourth Glorious Mystery
### *The Assumption of Mary into Heaven*

Pray the Our Father and consider this:

Be there when Mary, at the end of her earthly life, is taken body and soul to the glory of heaven, the reward of leading a life of total fidelity to God's will and purity of body and soul. See how the angels escort her to paradise and listen to their song: "Arise, my friend, my beautiful one, and come! For see, the winter is past, the rains are over and gone" (Song of Songs 2:10–11). Look at how lovely she is and feel her infinite joy at being reunited with her dearly beloved Son in the glory of heaven.

As you pray the ten Hail Marys, rejoice with Mary as you contemplate her glorious assumption. Share in her incomparable gladness as she embraces Jesus again in heaven. In praise and wonder, end with the Glory Be.

## Fifth Glorious Mystery
### *The Coronation of Mary as Queen of Heaven and Earth*

Pray the Our Father and consider this:

Join in the joy of the entire heavenly court as they welcome Mary into the presence of the Holy Trinity. Behold how beautiful and radiant she is as she is crowned by the Father, Son, and Holy Spirit as Queen of Heaven and Earth. Hear the saints and angels sing as she is given a place beside her Son. From her place in heaven, Mary continues to intercede for us, her children, here on earth. As she did at Cana, our Mother is quick to feel our pain and sense our needs, which she promptly brings before the throne of God.

As you pray the ten Hail Marys, bask in the glory of the Holy Trinity in the heavenly court as Mary is crowned Queen. Join her in praise and thanksgiving to God for all the wonders he has fulfilled in her life and in yours. Lift up, through her intercession, whatever needs or concerns you have at this moment. In worship and adoration, end with the Glory Be.

# Concluding Prayers

## TRIPLE COLLOQUY (THREEFOLD CONVERSATION)

Ignatius recommends concluding each prayer period with a triple colloquy or threefold conversation with our Lady, Jesus, and the Father—one in which we communicate whatever is in our heart at the end of our time in contemplation.

The conversation is made by opening your heart candidly, as one friend speaks to another, as children chat with parents, or as brothers talk with sisters. After speaking, also try to listen with a heart that is open to whatever response or invitation may be offered. Some possible points for the conversation may be:

- *How did you feel or what did you realize during your prayer?*

- *What struck you or touched you most?*

- *Do you want to ask or say anything now?*

- *Is there anything that our Father, Jesus, or our Lady want to say to you?*

- *Is there anything they are asking of you or telling you to do?*

At this point, take some time to personally converse with Mary, then with Jesus, and then with the Father, before ending the rosary in the usual way.

## THE HAIL HOLY QUEEN

Hail, holy Queen, mother of mercy,
our life, our sweetness, and our hope.
To thee do we cry, poor banished children
  of Eve;
to thee do we send up our sighs,
mourning and weeping in this valley of tears.
Turn, then, most gracious advocate,
thine eyes of mercy toward us;
and after this, our exile,
show unto us the blessed fruit of thy womb,
  Jesus.
O clement, O loving, O sweet Virgin Mary.

## THE LITANY OF
## THE BLESSED VIRGIN MARY

Optional but recommended especially on Marian feasts and solemnities:

Lord, have mercy on us.
   Christ, have mercy on us.

Lord, have mercy on us. Christ hear us.
   Christ, graciously hear us.

God the Father of heaven,
   Have mercy on us.

God the Son, Redeemer of the world,
   Have mercy on us.

God the Holy Spirit,
   Have mercy on us.

Holy Trinity, one God,
   Have mercy on us.


Holy Mary, pray for us.
Holy Mother of God, pray for us.
Holy Virgin of virgins, pray for us.
Mother of Christ, pray for us.
Mother of the Church, pray for us.

Mother of mercy, pray for us.
Mother of divine grace, pray for us.
Mother of hope, pray for us.
Mother most pure, pray for us.
Mother most chaste, pray for us.
Mother inviolate, pray for us.
Mother undefiled, pray for us.
Mother most amiable, pray for us.
Mother most admirable, pray for us.
Mother of good counsel, pray for us.
Mother of our Creator, pray for us.
Mother of our Savior, pray for us.
Virgin most prudent, pray for us.
Virgin most venerable, pray for us.
Virgin most renowned, pray for us.
Virgin most powerful, pray for us.
Virgin most merciful, pray for us.
Virgin most faithful, pray for us.
Mirror of justice, pray for us.
Seat of wisdom, pray for us.
Cause of our joy, pray for us.
Spiritual vessel, pray for us.
Vessel of honor, pray for us.
Singular vessel of devotion, pray for us.
Mystical rose, pray for us.

Tower of David, pray for us.

Tower of ivory, pray for us.

House of gold, pray for us.

Ark of the covenant, pray for us.

Gate of heaven, pray for us.

Morning star, pray for us.

Health of the sick, pray for us.

Refuge of sinners, pray for us.

Solace of migrants, pray for us.

Comforter of the afflicted, pray for us.

Help of Christians, pray for us.

Queen of Angels, pray for us.

Queen of Patriarchs, pray for us.

Queen of Prophets, pray for us.

Queen of Apostles, pray for us.

Queen of Martyrs, pray for us.

Queen of Confessors, pray for us.

Queen of Virgins, pray for us.

Queen of all Saints, pray for us.

Queen conceived without original sin, pray for us.

Queen assumed into heaven,

Queen of the most holy rosary, pray for us.

Queen of Families, pray for us.

Queen of Peace, pray for us.

Lamb of God, you take away the sins of the world,
    Spare us, O Lord.

Lamb of God, you take away the sins of the world,
    Graciously hear us, O Lord.

Lamb of God, you take away the sins of the world,
    Have mercy on us.

# FINAL PRAYER

**V.** Pray for us, O holy Mother of God,

**R.** That we may be made worthy of the promises of Christ.

Let us pray:

O God, whose only begotten Son, by his life, death, and resurrection has purchased for us the rewards of eternal life, grant, we beseech Thee, that meditating upon these mysteries of the Most Holy Rosary of the Blessed Virgin Mary, we may imitate what they contain and obtain what they promise, through the same Christ Our Lord. Amen.

**V.** May the divine assistance remain always with us.

**R.** Amen.

**V.** May the souls of the faithful departed through the mercy of God rest in peace.

**R.** Amen.

**V.** And may the blessing of Almighty God, the Father and the Son and the Holy Spirit, descend upon us and remain with us always.

**R.** Amen.

## PRAYER TO ST. JOSEPH

This prayer was composed by Pope Leo XIII in his 1889 encyclical. He asked that it be added at the end of the rosary, especially during the month of October, which is traditionally dedicated to the rosary (On Devotion to St. Joseph [*Quamquam Pluries*], 6).

To you, O blessed Joseph,
   do we come in our tribulation,
   and having implored the help of your
      most holy Spouse,
   we confidently invoke your patronage also.

Through that charity which bound you
   to the Immaculate Virgin Mother of God
   and through the paternal love
   with which you embraced the Child Jesus,
   we humbly beg you graciously to regard
      the inheritance
   which Jesus Christ has purchased by
      his Blood,
   and with your power and strength to aid
      us in our necessities.

O most watchful guardian of the Holy Family,
   defend the chosen children of Jesus Christ;
   O most loving father, ward off from us
   every contagion of error and corrupting
      influence;
   O our most mighty protector, be kind to us
   and from heaven assist us in our struggle
   with the power of darkness.

As once you rescued the Child Jesus from
      deadly peril,
   so now protect God's Holy Church
   from the snares of the enemy and from all
      adversity;
   shield, too, each one of us by your
      constant protection,
   so that, supported by your example and
      your aid,
   we may be able to live piously, to die
      in holiness,
   and to obtain eternal happiness in heaven.

Amen.

## NEW INVOCATIONS
## TO THE LITANY OF ST. JOSEPH

The Vatican added seven new invocations to the Litany of St. Joseph on the feast of St. Joseph the Worker, May 1, 2021. These are the first changes to the litany since its original promulgation in 1909.

The wording was drawn from the writings of various popes as they reflected on St. Joseph and his role in the universal Church. Pope Francis approved the invocations, which were presented to him by the Vatican Congregation for Divine Worship and the Discipline of the Sacraments.

The new invocations are prayed as follows:

*Guardian of the Redeemer*, pray for us.
*Servant of Christ*, pray for us.
*Minister of salvation*, pray for us.
*Support in difficulties*, pray for us.
*Patron of exiles*, pray for us.
*Patron of the afflicted*, pray for us.
*Patron of the poor*, pray for us.